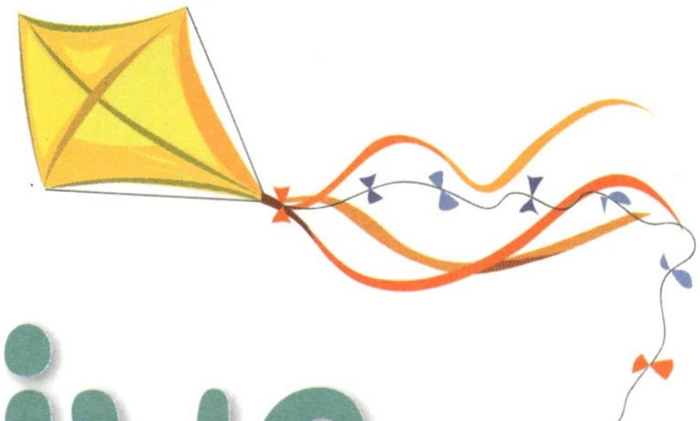

Creative Writing

Workbook 4

Om KIDZ
An imprint of Om Books International

Write an informative essay about your favourite place.

Your favourite place could be a beach, a park or even your own room. It could also be an imaginary place. Write what makes it special and why you love it more than other places.

NEW NEIGHBOURS

Imagine that a new family has come to live in the house next to yours. Write a story about them.

You can give each member of the family a quirky personality. You could make your story funny or serious.

GAME TIME

Have you tried any extreme sport? Like sky diving or para sailing? Write a few lines about an extreme sport you would like to try and why.

Write a brief introduction on how you got to know about the game. Explain the game and end your essay by describing why you like it.

SAVE NATURE

Let us take everyone on an antipollution drive. Write five things you would do to help reduce pollution.

Here are some clues.
Reduce, Recycle and Reuse.

Write your headline here.

Write a few lines on how trees can be saved.

GENIE JOY

Imagine you rubbed a magic lamp and a genie appeared. What would you wish for and why?

Would you be scared if a genie suddenly appeared?

LETTER OF LEAVE

Imagine that you needed to take 15 days off from school. Write a formal letter to your principal asking for permission.

Your address
____

____

____

Date
____

The Principal

Address
____

____

Subject: ____

Dear Sir/Madam,

____

____

____

Your sincerely,

____

Keep the tone respectful. Explain the reason behind your leave and describe how you plan to catch up with the classes you will miss.

GET WELL SOON

Have you visited an ailing friend or relative in a large hospital? Write about your visit.

If you haven't been to a hospital, read about it on the Internet and create a story about the visit. Describe the surroundings, the people you are likely to meet and how you would feel about it.

MY COUNTRY

Write an informative essay about your country.

Begin by stating facts like its capital and national symbols. Describe a few fascinating places in your country and write about the things that make it unique.

TREE TALK

Imagine a conversation between two tall trees on an island. Write it in a dialogue form below.

Think of the story you want to tell before you begin writing. Adapt this story in a dialogue format.

CHOCOLATE FACTORY

Imagine that you are visiting a chocolate factory with your best friend. Write a story about the adventure you had there.

Describe the factory and the things you saw. Weave your adventure around it. Add a dash of suspense and stir up a pot of chocolate surprises!

LAUGH OUT LOUD

Imagine that you are a comedian. Prepare a speech for your act. Include as many jokes as you can.

Look at the events happening around you. You might have something funny to say about them. Keep the jokes light and funny. Remember: Your jokes should not hurt someone's feelings.

Level 4

KITCHEN SECRETS

What would a perfect sandwich taste like?
Write the recipe for it.

A recipe must have a list of ingredients and step-by-step instructions that tell you how to make the dish. If it involves using the stove, ask an adult to help you write the recipe.

TRAVELOGUE

Imagine that you are travelling to a place far away from home. Write an informative essay about your journey.

FEARSOME FOES

What scares you the most? Write an essay about your deepest, darkest fear.

Describe the thing that scares you most and write why you are so scared of it. It could be ghosts, spiders, snakes or anything else that has you cowering in fright.

CITY OF DREAMS

Imagine that you landed in a magical city unlike anything you can ever find on this planet. Write a story about this city.

Give the city a name. Describe it. Create a story about your visit there. You may even use these pictures as clues.

AFTERSCHOOL ADVENTURES

What do you like to do once you are home from school? Write a diary entry about it.

A diary entry is written in first person. You could write about the people you interact with, the activities you do and the things you like doing.

CAMPING CAPERS

Have you ever been on a camping trip with your friends or family? Write about your camping adventure.

One usually camps by a water body or in a forest. Describe your surroundings and the things you did with your friends. Your experience could be pleasant or unpleasant.

SWEET SIBLING

Write a song or poem for your sibling or cousin.

Include a message in your song. It could be as simple as thanking your sibling for being a part of your life.

MOVIE MAGIC

When was the last time you went to the movies? Write an essay about it.

Describe the movie theatre. Write a paragraph describing the film you watched there. Talk about the people around you and the snacks you ate too.

TRAFFIC JAM

Imagine the thoughts going through the people's minds when they are stuck in a traffic jam. Look at these people and write their thoughts.

Try and think of a story for each character before you write. Create an imaginary destination for them. This will help you write their thoughts.

SCHOOL BUS

TABLE MANNERS

What are good table manners? Make a poster telling your friends about them.

Write your headline here.

____

____

Draw a picture in the middle.

Write your rules.

____

____

____

____

____

____

____

____

IF I WERE A SQUIRREL

What would you do if you were a squirrel? Write a poem about it!

Squirrels like to hop from tree to tree and gather nuts. Try to include these features in your poem.

LETTER TO THE MAYOR

The traffic signal in your area is not working. Write a letter to the mayor of your city, asking him or her to look into the matter.

Explain how it has disrupted the traffic in the area and the problems it is causing. Request the mayor to resolve the problem as soon as possible.

Your address
____

____

Date
____

The Principal

Address
____

____

Subject: ________________________

Dear Sir/Madam,

____

____

____

Your sincerely,

____

THUMBTACK TALES

Write an autobiography of a thumbtack.

A thumbtack is used to pin papers to a soft-board. Imagine its journey as you write its story.

NIGHT OF TERRORS

Write a horror story about a windy night.

Suspense is the key element in a horror story. Describe the sounds of the wind, build anticipation and make every little aspect sound mysterious and spooky.

ACROSTIC ADVENTURES

An acrostic poem is a fun way to write a poem. Look at the example below and create your own acrostic poem.

Write any word vertically (in a top to bottom arrangement). Think of words or phrases that start with each letter of that word. You can also use rhyming words to make your poem musical.

Apples are juicy

Pretty, red and yummy

Pick when they are ripe

Let them fill up your tummy

Eat them day and night